# Paddington's ABC

## by Michael Bond

### Illustrated by John Lobban

#### Devised by Carol Watson

## COLLINS

William Collins Sons & Co Ltd
London · Glasgow · Sydney · Auckland
Toronto · Johannesburg

First published 1990
© Michael Bond 1990
© illustrations Wm Collins Sons & Co Ltd 1990

A CIP catalogue record for this book is available from the British Library

ISBN 0 00 185115 2

Printed and bound in Portugal by Resopal.
This book is set in Century Schoolbook

# Aa

apple

# Bb

boots

# Cc

camera

# Dd

duck

# Ee

egg

# Ff

fence

# Gg

ghost

# Hh

hat

# Ii

# ink

# Jj

BEST
MARMALADE

jar

# Kk

kite

# Ll

Please look after this BEAR. THANK YOU.

label

# Mm

marmalade

# N n

net

# Oo

# ostrich

# P p

pyjamas

# Qq

queen

# Rr

rake

# Ss

# suitcase

# Tt

# telephone

# U u

# umbrella

# V v

## violin

# Ww

wall

# Xx

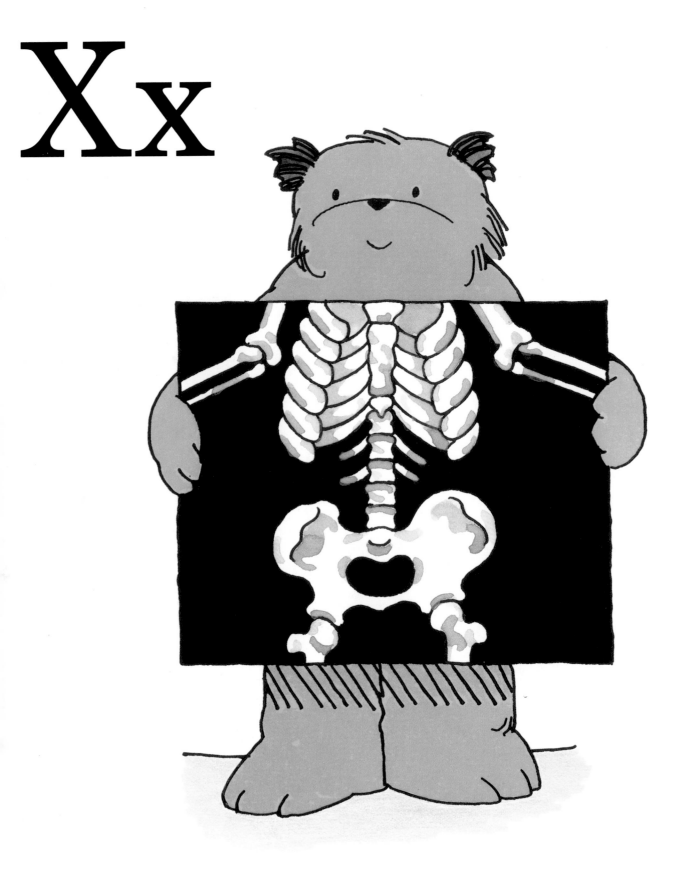

# x-ray

# Yy

yo-yo

# Zz

zebra

How many things can you see which begin with s?

Do you know what letter is missing
from the beginning of these words?

.......... pple

......... gg

.......... ence

......... nk

.........at

.........all

.........oots

.........et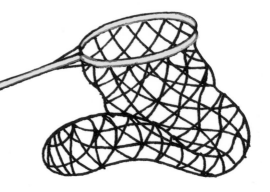

# The alphabet

Aa Bb Cc

Dd Ee Ff Gg

Hh Ii Jj Kk

Ll Mm Nn

Oo Pp Qq

Rr Ss Tt

Uu Vv Ww

Xx Yy Zz